The 7-O's

of Sales

The Intentional Experience

By: Edward A. Earle

INTRODUCTION

I remember the development history of this unique and amazingly effective and efficient sales format I developed called the 7 O's of Sales... The Intentional Experience.

The reason I'm taking this approach to explaining my concept of the 7 O's of Sales... The Intentional Experience is because I know that you are probably familiar with many of the sales trainers, authors and consultants who are out there today or who have been in the past.

You've probably read some of their books, listened to some of their audio programs, or attended some of their seminars. Perhaps you have brought some of them in to work directly with your organization.

I don't know about you, but when I first started selling, I did those same exact things.

I bought every book, listened to every sales tape (back then they were all tapes) and went to all kinds of sales seminars... and the thing that kept sticking out in my mind, the thing I kept saying to myself was, *"I wonder if these so called sales trainers, who are supposed to be the best in the world, I wonder if they can actually SELL?"*

Selling... in the same way that I was selling every day. Selling... the same way that the sales professionals who I was competing against every day were selling. Selling... the same way that YOU and your competitors are selling every day. SELLING.

I wondered how successful they were at actually SELLING real products and services... selling things besides their own books and tapes.

We just never seemed to know about their real background in sales. We never knew what they used to sell before they became this so-called *world-renowned sales authority.*

That always left me wondering as to the credibility and actual experience that these sales experts truly possessed.

That also made me suspect if they were really experts at all – or if they were just really good speakers, orators or presenters, which is fine... but makes me question the validity of their information as well as their approach to sales.

I don't know about you, but to me, in the end this is all about money.

It's all about my money... my income... my lifestyle. The last thing I want is to be in front of a great prospect trying a technique advocated by one of these experts... only to have it backfire on me.

What's the old Chinese proverb?

"Never mess with another man's rice bowl."

I want to give you some insight as to the actual events that led up to this amazing sales process I call the 7 O's of Sales... The Intentional Experience.

And with that as a backdrop, let's get started.

Chapter One

Sitting At A Different Table

"When you sit with winners, the conversations are different."

— Dawn Madison

At the time of its initial inspiration and creation, I was a business development consultant, focusing mainly on marketing, advertising and sales.

Companies of all sizes paid me to implement within their companies my 3-D approach to marketing, which was to Devise, Deploy and Defend new and innovative marketing strategies.

And since I was very successful at what I did, this allowed them to rapidly increase their sales and their market share.

I was working on behalf of a client in the banking industry. They were building a nationwide infrastructure of entrepreneurs to market and represent products and services for their new small business division.

I was helping them recruit these entrepreneurs all across the United States.

Potential entrepreneurs would respond to advertising and then at the beginning of a given week, would come to an opportunity and investment meeting and presentation at a nice hotel.

I would give the presentation and then conduct appointments and interviews with qualified individuals throughout the balance of the week.

At the time, each entrepreneur's investment was around $15,000. For our success, we were commissioned at about $4,000 for each new investment partner recruited with additional

bonuses based on the number of partners recruited.

Before I got involved with this company, there were already four other presenters on the road conducting these events. They were having the amount of success typical for that type of sales structure.

Their presenters were top-notch, seasoned professionals who had worked for some big-pitch firms before they came to work here.

They were trained, they were aggressive, and they knew how to ask questions. They knew consultative selling and tie-downs. They knew how to overcome objections, ask for the order and then shut up. In essence, these guys were good.

And I, myself, was no slouch. I had studied and practiced sales for years. I had been to every legitimate sales training, read every book and listened to every tape and CD.

Yet even with all of that experience, this company was struggling to get into the black. As a matter of fact, they were growing so fast that they were almost out of business.

Their sales success was just good enough to keep them expanding, but not good enough to close more of the prospects they saw and not good enough to boost their investment price.

They needed to leverage their sales opportunities.

The problem was that the sales paradigm had shifted. The rules of the game had changed.

The sales training and skills that we all knew then and know to this day didn't apply any more. The days of simple selling had come to an end.

And one of the rules of a paradigm is that when a paradigm shifts, everyone goes back to ZERO.

Let's talk about this for a little bit. This concept of the paradigm shifting is extremely significant and I don't want you to gloss over it without giving it intense consideration.

Let's talk about the words "paradigm" and "shift" in more detail.

The word paradigm first appeared in English in the 15th century, meaning, "set as an example, pattern or model."

The word Paradigm also means "A set of assumptions, concepts, values, and practices that constitutes a way of viewing reality for the community that shares them, especially in an intellectual discipline."

Think about that for a minute. A sales paradigm then, is a set of assumptions, sales concepts, values, and sales practices (techniques, training, methods) that constitutes a way of viewing

"reality," or how real success in sales is achieved for the community that shares them, in this case businesses and their salespeople, especially in an intellectual discipline.

The sales paradigm is the discipline of selling customers or of getting people to buy what you sell.

A paradigm is a reality. We rely on it every day for our success and perpetuation. Everything we do is based on those assumptions and those patterns because they are seemingly uniform, unfaltering and unfailing.

So, when a paradigm shifts or changes... WOW! That causes a massive quagmiric riddle, which doesn't just frustrate the processes and the results.

Not just that...

Everything just comes to an immediate, screeching halt.

The reason?

A shift is to put (something) aside and replace it by another or others;

change, exchange or substitute. So in the end, a shift in the paradigm means that the assumptions, concepts, values, practices and patterns that we have come to depend on to create a specific result (in this case sales) has been replaced, changed, exchanged and substituted with another completely different set of assumptions, concepts, values, practices and patterns.

In essence, we as a business community, whether you are a company, a salesperson or a sales trainer or author, are following old assumptions, values, concepts practices and patterns.

And they just don't apply any more.

They have been substituted and replaced. This is why everyone goes back to ZERO when a paradigm shifts. Nobody knows the new patterns and nobody knows the rules.

And it affects everyone.

This is the reason that almost every sales book you read, or seminar you attend, or trainer you hire will most always be ineffective.

They are teaching you assumptions, values, concepts, practices and patterns that are no longer valid. That have been replaced or substituted by new ones.

And to make matters worse, the sales industry is not only one, but it is two major paradigm shifts behind.

The result is that the prospects and the marketplace stop responding. Sales results go down and start flailing.

The numbers are off – they're way off.

It's harder to get a prospect on the phone, harder to get in the door, harder to gain their trust, harder to keep them from only

looking at the bottom line (or what I call the "Last Page Lump Sum").

It's harder to position yourself against your competition without being negative, harder to keep from being out-negotiated, harder to keep your margins, harder to get the deal closed without giving too many concessions.

It's harder to keep from chasing the sale for days, weeks, months, etc., and harder to maintain control of the whole thing.

And, unfortunately, with a paradigm shift, it's not going to get better.

If you, your company or your salespeople are selling based on old sales training – and technically most current sales trainings and philosophies are based and grounded in the old sales paradigm, they just throw in new presenters and packaging – no matter how much time or money you have invested... it will not work.

The rules have changed and you are fouling out every time and you, like this client of mine at the time, just don't know why.

The 7 O's of Sales... The Intentional Experience is based on the new paradigm.

I will personally teach you the new assumptions, values, concepts, practices and patterns you need in order to be hugely successful in anything you sell.

So back to my story...

I knew that I had to change something. I knew that the paradigm had shifted from sales.

It's what my first book was all about. Ushering in the new paradigm.

My entire prior company was based on knowing how to compensate for and ultimately fix this paradigm shift away from simple selling.

But I had been accomplishing that through marketing and advertising-based solutions. At the time I had not yet developed it into a sales format.

I guess it was time to do that.

The problem, though, was how to create a sales format that met a seemingly impossible, long list of requirements.

The format had to be universal so that any type of company in any industry could use it to sell to any type of company or customer in any type of industry.

It had to be universal so that any salesperson, regardless of industry, background, experience level, skill base, personality strengths or weaknesses, age, education or environment could implement it and have significantly greater success.

It had to be systematic in its approach so it could be replicated and duplicated easily throughout an organization and instantly measurable by the individual salesperson and management.

It had to easily expose flaws in presentation so they could immediately be corrected in order to keep sales numbers at their peak.

It had to compensate for the fact that every customer is different. They have different backgrounds and different personality profiles.

They each value different things and have different ways of being approached, and they have different temperaments regardless of their title or the type of company they work for.

It had to build on a salesperson's strengths, yet compensate for the inherent weaknesses in their personality profile... and it had to somehow do that without asking them to drastically change their human nature!

In this way, a very open and communicative salesperson could sell to a very analytical and facts and process-oriented prospect and still have great success.

So, just how do you know the profile of each prospect?

Do you ask them to do an executive psych evaluation before your sales appointment so you can send a salesperson who has matching values and approaches (read humor!)?

All of this is dependent upon the fact that you believe that this concept is valid and that you even know the profile of your own salespeople.

(By the way, I conduct that executive DISC profile analysis for everyone who attends the 7 O's Sales Training Program.)

It had to set up the salesperson to have control over the sales situation right from the very beginning.

And all of the information that needed to be communicated had to be communicated in the right order... without the prospects jumping ahead or disrespectfully interrupting with questions or objections.

It had to allow the customers to become collaborative with their concerns instead of tackling the situation with tension-caused tirades.

It had to somehow get the prospects to willingly and excitedly offer up their greatest weaknesses and their true desires for the outcome.

And it had to do that without hiding those weaknesses and desires behind a wall of due diligence officers designed to protect the actual decision-makers.

There are so many things I wanted this process of mine, my new creation, to accomplish. There were so many things that this new sales process

of mine "HAD" to accomplish. The list can go on and on. But one of my main objectives was that I wanted the customers to chase me.

I wanted them to ask me if they could buy.

This was critical to me because I know that most top-notch, assertive, "type A" salespeople are extremely difficult to find.

And in today's "Entrepreneurial Age," many of those top-notch salespeople have gone into business for themselves.

Wouldn't you agree that if there's a labor shortage across the board, in every department and every skill, then there's definitely a sales personnel drought?

Wouldn't you also agree that it's not getting any better?

I have identified 15 main reasons for this famine of those who make sales their forte:

1. There are very few good places to learn

2. It takes a lot of years of knowledge and
hard work to be good

3. There's a negative attitude and perception towards the sales profession; it's seen as "The job you take when you can't get anything else better"

4. Used car salesman perception – it's your first thought when you think about salespeople

5. Negative experiences

6. Intelligent people are generally more perceptive to rejection

7. Professors promote this negative attitude toward sales

8. Media reinforces the stereotype

9. Except for a few professions (Real Estate, insurance, etc.), it's not a licensed profession

10. Good salespeople are almost always promoted to management

11. "Bad Golfer syndrome" – the perpetuation of bad selling habits due to lack of training from the start

12. It takes considerable patience – especially if the sale is more complex

13. Rewards are not guaranteed – full commission

14. Technical Sales: Very few people have the combination of expertise and sales soft skills – this requires a real unique person

15. Companies really minimize the importance of sales, their salespeople, training, etc.; they don't even realize that they are a "sales" driven organization

The idea that was once held that if you want to make money, get into sales. This idea has been not just been tarnished, it has almost been replaced.

Replaced? But, by what?

I believe it has been replaced by the concept of what I call "e-teen-preneurs," extremely young (barely out of their teenage years), computer savvy and very ballsy kids making millions and billions of dollars.

This is what people are aspiring to.

The perception seems to have become that the Big Money revolves around computers, web software development, etc. and things like that, but surely not sales skills.

The days of sales greatness have ended. Trying to find great salespeople has become more and more difficult, if not next to impossible.

When it comes to getting quality salespeople, you don't attract them. You don't find them. You don't run ads and have them call. You don't call a recruiter and have them start sending resumes.

Finding top salespeople essentially requires an all out marketing and sales program.

Funny huh? A complete marketing and "sales" program to find top quality "sales" people. And as silly as it sounds, it's absolutely true.

The facts are the facts.

[QUICK SIDE NOTE: I have developed such a program and I will allow you to access and implement it free of charge within your

organization. It really works magic when it comes to developing a strong sales force.]

So, because of this shortage of salespeople with the courage to withstand a customer's objections and still ask for the full order, I wanted a sales format which would naturally cause the customer to *ask me for the order*, since I knew that most salespeople wouldn't do it.

In the end, it was a really big list of requirements that I had placed on this new sales process.

It really seemed to be impossible to fill or to even think that developing such a sales process was at all possible.

Up until that point, there has never been a sales process with all of those advantages and rewards ever created by any sales author, trainer or company.

As a matter of fact, truth be told, that includes pretty much all the sales trainers and sales programs which I had looked into.

None of them address this basic fundamental problem of the paradigm shift, not to mention the many other issues that make their programs null and void.

And this is not just my opinion; it's not my attempt to badmouth or bash my competition. (I don't consider other trainers or philosophies competition.)

This is the opinion of tens of thousands of small- to mid-sized growth oriented companies and CEO's and their sales managers; the people I work with every day.

These are the opinions of the people who read the books, attend the seminars, buy the CD sets at the back of the room, pay gobs of money (sometimes as much as the cost of a home) to send their people to prominent sales programs with the end result being... no increase in performance whatsoever.

The bottom-line?

Two days of production lost and tens of thousands of dollars, if not significantly more, wasted.

Their feeling?

The program wasn't customized for their company's specific needs. The program and

system were difficult to internalize and implement. They still had no ability to manage the new format because of lack of expertise within their company.

I feel the same way. It seems that the better a sales training program claims to be, in reality, the more complex it is.

The seductive secrets of accelerated swells of sales always seem to be stymied by a pseudo-sophisticated structure or system.

In other words: *"Whaddya say there, Jeb? I caint understand ya."* (redneck drawl!)

Think about all of the problems that exist within a typical sales situation.

When it comes to prospecting, how do you get in the door?

How do you really know if the prospect is actually truly qualified?

Or before your sales meeting, how many competitors have been there before you?

How many are coming in after you? What are they saying?

How have the prospects been preparing for you or this sales presentation?

Who are they asking for advice and what advice are they getting?

During the actual meeting there is a high level of tension and distrust. You don't really know what the prospect is thinking and sometimes the prospect can be aggressive and resistant.

How do you read everyone's body language?

How do you stop them from shortcutting to price, objections or other conversation?

How do you keep everyone's attention?

Do your prospects ever mentally wander during your presentation or ever get distracted by the every day duties of the business or life (which are difficult for them to ignore)?

How do you get everyone to "buy in?"

How do you keep the objections under control?

How do you get them to voice their concerns at the right and proper time... and stop interrupting your presentation?

How do you keep them from becoming hostile?

Or, keep what I call their "ringer rival" under control or even in your pocket? (You know the "ringer rival?" It's that internal or external influencer whispering in your prospect's ear.)

When it comes to the close, how do you avoid that awkward moment?

How do you know when to close?

What if the prospect shows strong buying signals or shows real signs of excitement. Do you "go in" for the close?

What do you do with other people who are involved in the decision?

What about stall tactics? How do you deal with negotiation tactics from the prospects?

What happens when they say they don't have the money?

Not to mention, what about after the sales meeting?

What happened right after the meeting? What were they thinking or saying?

Who else did they see and how did they feel about your competition?

What other prices or bids did they get?

How do you compete against an unknown?

How can you maintain your position and standing after you leave and during their deliberation period?

How do you get in on their deliberation process?

The list of problems is endless and is heightened by the differences in salespeople's personalities and experience; the prospect's personalities and experience; the industry, etc., and on and on.

You see?

There are so many complexities within a sale that it's easy for a training organization to get confused and try to address each of these problems.

The result is a sales training system that is quite overwhelming as well as difficult to remember, let alone use on the streets every day, where the rubber meets the road.

The crap is too hard! And if it's too hard, how will people use it?

They can't! Therefore there's no increase in sales performance.

I don't understand why this happens. I think when people in my industry don't really know the answers, they try to blindside and confuse the audience through what I call "Intellectual Intricacies."

In other words, they think, "If we can just sound smart or smarter than our clients and the businesses that are relying on us for good sales strategies, that's good enough. We make our money from speaking anyhow."

No one ever wants to look the fool.

And because people stop themselves from saying what's really on their mind – which is, *"Hey! This crap doesn't work!"* – sales authors and trainers get away with pawning off these "Cockeyed Counterfactual Conceptualisms" labeled as "Today's Hottest Sales Techniques."

It's just a different version of "The Emperor and His New Clothes."

These paper gurus are selling you – selling us – clothing made from invisible cloth. And here we are parading down Main Street stark naked in front of the entire kingdom!

Yet no one has the guts to say,

"Hey! Dude! YOU'RE NAKED!"

Except for me. I am the little boy in the story who speaks up.

Nonetheless, there are a couple of problems:

You ARE NAKED. The strategies don't work and your salespeople are out there in the marketplace with content that doesn't work.

You are parading around in front of the entire kingdom, every time you as a sales manager or organization "sell" your sales staff on training and it doesn't work – meaning they don't make more money. You are looking the fool's part. Your credibility is diminishing and dissolving.

And if you do this too many times (three to be exact)… VAMOOSE! Leadership credibility gone!

Now you have a bigger problem. Developing a great sales force isn't about sales management. To me, the concept of a sales manager is defective. It's about LEADERSHIP.

And when the leadership credibility has been forfeited carelessly, you have surely lost your power.

Now, why did I just state that the number of times you can offer bad training to your staff before you totally lose credibility is *three*?

It's what I have always called, the "Law of Global Conclusions."

A Global Conclusion is when people have determined that a certain thing, a certain person or idea is a certain way.

And that's the way it is... all of the time. Most of the time these are emotional conclusions and not based in any reality or fact.

Regardless, to the individual drawing the Global Conclusion, they are considered real and true.

Here's how the rule works:

If someone experiences something one time, they will conclude that "It just happens."

If they experience that situation two times, they will conclude that "It happens a lot."

And if they experience that situation three to four times, they will conclude that "It happens ALL OF THE TIME."

That is the "Law of Global Conclusions."

So if you have sponsored any sales training three times or more, a sales training that is supposed to help your sales staff make more money, and it has never panned out as promised, then your sales staff has drawn the Global Conclusion that _____. (You can fill in the statement yourself because chances are you have probably said it

yourself or have heard it said by other members of your team.)

People! Sales are easy.

Human beings are simple. There is no need for complexities. In the end, there is really no such thing as selling, and we all instinctively know this.

The whole concept is almost a relic, an antique.

Why? Because, the definition of the word "sell" is: To cause or persuade to accept; to convince.

Well, we never really sell because the customer has already mentally bought what you are supposedly "selling."

Think about this with me for just a minute.

If a prospect has called your company on the phone, or has come into your store, or has looked at your product or business online, or has fostered any type of activity, then he/she has already mentally bought.

Remember, the mind doesn't know the difference between reality and virtual reality.

If a prospect has already visualized the owning or using of your product or service in their mind – which by the way, if they are showing activity and interest at all that means they have – then in their mind, they have already bought.

They have already seen themselves enjoying the benefit.

There is no sale to be made. The sale, if any, is only "Who" and "When." "What model or service package" and "How much."

The selling has already been done by the prospect him or her self, so quit trying to sell.

And stop paying for training that tries to help you sell them! The deal is already in the "cup," so-to-speak.

Your job is just not to spill the deal out; the sale is already *a done deal* before you start "selling."

If you truly understand this, then the only thing left to do is hopefully instantly gain enough trust with the prospect so that you both can have a "Collaborative Conversation" about the details: the who (hopefully you), the when (hopefully now, especially within this pay period... right?) and how much (hopefully for you it's at full commission).

Remember the paradigm has changed and the marketplace is ready and willing to follow if someone (preferably you) would just lead the way.

To me a great sales process should be as simple as flicking on the light switch. It is easy and simple to do. Anyone can do it regardless of gender or age or experience.

The complexities of electricity and engineering are housed within the switch, so all we have to do is turn it on or turn it off. Sales should be the same way.

The 7 O's is that light switch.

So, when it came to developing this unique approach to sales – given the situation I was in with this banking client – I already had a very good idea about what needed to be done.

By now, most of the material was in my mind and I was already using a majority of it. I just needed to officially adapt it and then formalize the format and test it for success.

So let's talk about this process I developed.

First, let's talk about what I mean by the words The Intentional Experience.

Let's break down the words and I think you'll get a really good idea.

•**Intentional / Intention:** An act with an attitude predetermined to produce a result that affects another's actions or conduct.

•**Experience:** An undergoing of things occurring that are perceived, understood, and remembered.

So, if we combine those two definitions we get a better understanding of The Intentional Experience.

The Intentional Experience is then, a process that is created with the intention to produce a predetermined action or result in another person or persons that they cognitively perceive, understand, and remember.

That is exactly what the 7 O's of Sales is designed to do: create an Intentional Experience.

Everything we do and say is to create an experience and reflect reaction, an impulse with the prospect that overcomes every one of the problems we previously discussed with other methods of sales… and ultimately leads the prospect to ask us for the order.

This is very similar to a Broadway play or a great movie: everything from the dialogue, the tone of voice, the delivery, the actions, the props, the effects – everything.

In fact there are very many small and miniscule things that go into making that "one singular moment" in which the audience is moved to a specific predetermined emotional response.

It is the true art of making people do what you want them to do, when you want them to do it. You can make them cry, laugh, get angry... All at the same time.

You are in control.

Take for example the line in the movie Jerry Maguire, starring Tom Cruise as a sports agent and Renee Zellweger as his love interest.

"You had me at 'hello.'"

Just a simple line... only five little words. But the impact was huge.

That line MADE the movie. The line has become famous and a part of everyday culture. The line itself has become a massive brand.

Why? Why was it so powerful? It wasn't just the line itself. It was the set-up of the entire movie; every element came together for that one moment when Renee's character exclaimed, "You had me at hello."

Here's an example of a very simple phrase built on a few words that can change meaning depending on which word in the phrase you emphasize.

And if you say the phrase outlaid yourself emphasizing the specific words I highlight, you will see exactly what I mean and why understanding "words" and their power is so critical in sales.

"I Didn't Say You Stole. The Money."

"I Didn't Say You Stole The Money" is the phrase. Now I am going to write the phrase several times but each time with a different word highlighted and I want you to say the phrase out loud emphasizing the highlighted word. Got it?

First just read the phrase.

"I Didn't Say You Stole The Money."

Now read it each time with the emphasis on the highlighted word and notice how the phrase totally changes meaning.

"**I** Didn't Say You Stole The Money."

"I Didn't **Say** You Stole The Money."

"I Didn't Say **You** Stole The Money."

"I Didn't Say You **Stole** The Money."

"I Didn't Say You Stole The **Money**."

Now let me break it down a little based on how I explain it during the workshop.

"**I** Didn't Say You Stole The Money."

Comment: *You stole the money, I AM just not the one who said it.*

"I Didn't **Say** You Stole The Money."

Comment: *You stole the money, I just didn't SAY it... although I might have emailed or written a note.*

"I Didn't Say **You** Stole The Money."

Comment: *Someone stole the money, I just didn't say that it was YOU.*

"I Didn't Say You **Stole** The Money."

Comment: *The money is gone, I am just not saying that you STOLE it.*

"I Didn't Say You Stole The **Money**."

Comment: *You stole something, I am just not saying that it was MONEY.*

Can you see how differently the phrase becomes each time you emphasize a different word?

Are you a master of emphasis and words? Sales is not a game; there is no do-over button as there is on your kids' X-box.

You either have the skill to get the deal... or someone else gets it. Some other salesperson gets YOUR commission.

These are the techniques and principles I will teach you in the 7 O's of Sales... The Intentional Experience Training Program.

I will personally teach you how to be in total control of the sales outcome from beginning to end. You can just sit and watch your sales go through the roof... and your income along with it.

Now let's talk about the concept of the 7 O's of Sales themselves.

What are the seven O's and why the number seven? Let me address the concept behind the number seven and its significance in our lives and throughout history and the world.

You've heard the old saying that it takes 7 yeses (trial closes) to get the big yes (buying decision). Well, let's explore where that comes from and see why it has merit. Let's take a closer look at the symbolism of the number seven.

To begin with, there's the astronomical and religious calculation of old of the pagan Romans, who divided the week into *seven* days, and held the *seventh* day as the most sacred

The *seven* planets which are ever remaining at an equal distance from each other, and rotating in the same path, hence, the idea suggested by this motion, of the eternal harmony of the universe.

In the Hebrew language the number seven comes from the root word Sheva, which carries three fundamental meanings: The number seven; to be complete or full; and, to swear or take an oath.

The Pythagoreans considered the figure *seven* as the image and model of the divine order and harmony in nature.

If we follow these thoughts about symbolism of the number 7, then it is easy for us to understand that to our mind (worldwide, which is interestingly universal) the number

7 means that we are complete, full and at harmony.

When it comes to sales, it means that we have received enough information for our minds to say that the decision is good, which is why the old sales understanding is that if you can get seven yeses, you'll get the BIG YES.

The salesperson who understands the 7 O's of Sales... The Intentional Experience Sales Program will significantly increase their sales numbers, without every really having to "sell." I would know.

As the founder of the program, I have been often labeled as the *"True Greatest Salesman In The World."*

This title comes from having sold products and services in just about every industry, with a lifetime average conversion ratio of over 80%.

So, interestingly enough, the process of the prospect buying from you is broken down into seven components.

This is not me trying to force the actual process into my concept of seven; it just so happens that all of the natural components of a buying situation happen to equal seven parts. It's funny how it is that way.

It just reinforces the concept of how the mind actually functions when it relates to the symbolism of the number seven.

Here are the seven components... or the 7 O's of the sale.

What's the reason for the letter O? Just to make it easy to understand, learn and implement quickly:

O-1: Overview – Understand who the customer is, what they do, advantages they possess, disadvantages, competition, marketplace conditions, etc.

O-2: Objectives – Goals of the company/customer, current market share, conversion ratio, results desired, etc.

O-3: Obsolescence – What efforts have been made or are being made to reach objectives? What is not working and reasons why? Current statistics.

O-4: Opportunities – Your product or service presentation and how it meets the objectives; Return On Investment analysis.

O-5: Objections – This section is where the concerns and objections are voiced.

O-6: Zero Hour – Critical timeframes that affect the implementation or the result of the purchase.

O-7: Organize – Price, payment options, resources, plan for moving forward, etc.

During the training you'll be provided with a map of the 7 O's and we will customize your entire sales program wrapped around the principles of the 7 O's of Sales... The Intentional Experience.

You'll get everything from the opening dialogue of your salespeople, to their word tracks, actions, etc.

Everything is customized and then adapted to each of the attending salespeople. Why?

Because every salesperson is different, with different backgrounds and profiles.

We have to create the format so that it takes advantage of their strengths and provides support for their weaknesses.

This is something that you will never get at any other sales training program no matter how much you pay. This is not a "one-size-fits-all" kind of program.

Now back to my story of the origins of The Seven O's...

After I created the process, I was able to perfect it through a process that I call the Genesis Point.

I won't go through a significant amount of explanation about the Genesis Point Method on this short audio CD, mostly because of time restraints but also because I will cover it in detail and train you on this concept during the 7 O's Sales Training.

But the Genesis Point is a very unique meditation method that I had come across when I was 20 years old while studying with some psychiatrists from Rice University.

I had some interesting ideas about meditation as it related to the human psyche and the ability to change an individual's reality or perception in a very short period of time.

The purpose was to give people a tool that would allow them to create success in any area of their life.

A transformation of sorts... in an instant. A transfiguration – which is a transformation but not over time – in an instant.

I had been able to accomplish this massive change or transformation in my life in a 30-day period of time using this concept I now call the Genesis Point Method, and I wanted professional and scientific background on my ideas.

At the time of creating this new sales training format I knew that using the Genesis Point Method which I had developed years earlier would afford me the ability to perfect my format.

Here's why: What the Genesis Point allows me to do is create a virtual reality in the mind. It allowed me the ability to:

- Be the salesperson giving the sales presentation

- Be the customer or customers in the sales presentation

- Be a third party observer on the side of the sales presentation, all without having to physically be giving sales presentations.

What are the benefits? The program and process is simple and profound.

Let me explain:

If I went into the Genesis Point as a customer or any specific customer within a group (decision maker, financier, or influencers – internal or external) I could see myself as I gave the presentation and feel all of the feelings and emotions, and think the thoughts of those customers.

Instantly I knew that as a customer I was or was not believing or trusting. I literally had become the customer.

Please stay with me here.

This is a very powerful technique you won't find anywhere else and it has allowed me probably the highest sales conversion ratio in the industry, selling every type of service or product all over the world.

If I went into the Genesis Point as the Virtual Trainer, I was able to observe me as the salesperson with the customer or group of customers... and the interaction between us. I caught – because I was there for – every interaction between the two parties.

I became aware of tons of little things that a salesperson would miss while he or she was focusing on correctly delivering his or her presentation, not to mention the coping with the enormous amount of stress a salesperson feels when a commission is on the line.

By using the Genesis Point Method looking at it from these two perspectives, I could make notes as it related to my performance as a salesperson.

Was I coming across the right way?

Was the customer on board with me?

Was he lying to me, telling me one thing but thinking another?

Was I influencing them?

Were they actually really excited to buy but didn't want to disclose that fact so they didn't appear too anxious or hoped maybe could get my product for less?

There are so many things I could find out by using the Genesis Point Method.

Then I could take notes and go back to the 7 O's of Sales Process and Format and look at what I was doing wrong.

I could make those fixes or repairs and then go back to the Genesis Point Method as the salesperson and practice these repairs.

I could keep using the Genesis Point Method as these three individuals (salesperson, customer, virtual trainer) until I perfected my sales ability and the 7 O's format.

I could work within the Genesis Point until I was getting the result I wanted from the customer, which is a customer who trusted me and would ask me for the order.

I really have no ability to explain the power of this technique. But I can say that after two days with me, for the companies and salespeople who have attended my 7 O's Sales Training and then utilized the Genesis Point Method, those folks have come out with a huge increase in their sales results.

They make way more money as a salesperson and their companies make more money.

Outside of the serious advantages I just outlined, one of the biggest reasons I use the Genesis Point Method in perfecting a salesperson's skill is that as an entrepreneur, business owner, C-Level executive just like you, I hate – absolutely hate – salespeople practicing on what I call "Live Leads."

The last thing I want, and hopefully you can identify with me here, is handing over leads, for which I have paid a lot of money, to inexperienced or even *less* experienced salespeople.

You tell me: don't you want to give all of your leads to your top closer?

You know that if you could give every lead to your top closer you would make a lot more money.

Problem: you only have one top closer and too many leads. So, naturally, the weaker salespeople have to get some of them. But really what's worse here is that we train salespeople on "Live Leads."

We let them BURN leads. How?

When they can't close as high as your best guy, they BURN the leads.

You've wasted your money and gotten nothing in return.

That is, provided that your best guy is even really good enough to earn the title "Best" or "Top." I guess it's all relative.

If you are training sales personnel on Live Leads you are burning money... and I can't stand the idea of a salesperson leaving a deal for my competitor to walk by and pick up.

It drives me insane... and it should you, also!

From this point on, using the Genesis Point Method along with the 7 O's will stop this from ever happening to your organization.

As Alec Baldwin's character (a top salesman and now manager) screamed to the lagging sales staff in the 1992 movie, Glengarry Glen Ross, "Coffee's for closers!"

Well so are leads. Leads are for closers only... PERIOD! NO EXCEPTIONS!

During the 7 O's Sales Training, I'll teach my very powerful Genesis Point Method.

As a matter of fact, your salespeople will use my Genesis Point technique throughout the training program to analyze their current format of selling, customize the 7 O's structure to your specific organization and marketplace... and then realize the results by perfecting the structure before they leave.

The results will be that your people will go back to your organization tuned and ready to make more sales and more money.

Which is the entire point... right?

Now that I have given you a little understanding on the process and performance of my very unique sales approach called the 7 O's of Sales... The Intentional Experience, let me conclude by telling the rest of the story about how the approach worked for me the very first time I put it into place in my own personal sales efforts.

I remember the experience so vividly and it sticks out in my mind as the catalytical experience and one of the most defining moments in my professional career... not to mention the gigantic leap in my personal income and confidence in my ability to make more money than seemed normally possible.

The night before the next sales day, I was excited. I knew this new approach was going to work.

I don't know why I felt that way.

I think that because of the Genesis Point concept I had been engaged in, I had seemed to have "been there" or "here" before.

I just knew.

The next morning I started my appointments. As the first prospect was introduced and sat down, I began the meeting with an opening dialogue

that I now call "The Magic Mouth." This is an opening dialogue to every sales situation for any sales person with any background in any industry.

This opening dialogue is based on the 7 O's and when used, essentially allows a salesperson to get the seven "yeses" that he or she needs from the prospect to pave the way for the final BIG YES.

The most impressive part of this Magic Mouth opening dialogue is that it is accomplished in the first 30 seconds of any sales situation.

I can't even begin to describe the benefits, but there is a reason that I call it the Magic Mouth. Just using the dialogue alone will double your or your company's sales closing ratio or percentage *within the first day*.

I have the data to back up that statement.

At my 7 O's of Sales... The Intentional Experience, I will train you and every single one of your salespeople to be proficient with the use of the Magic Mouth... before they leave the program.

You will start closing more deals and making more money RIGHT NOW!

So, that morning, as soon as I started talking through the Magic Mouth opening dialog with my first prospect, I felt him buying into the process.

I felt him hand me total control and surrender to me.

I watched as his head nodded in agreement, and heard him say "yes" to each of the points in my Magic Mouth opening dialogue.

After the first 30 seconds, I followed the 7 O's process right down the line.

And I must tell you that I wasn't even perfect at the execution.

I know it was a little rough, but I followed my 7 O's structure.

As I walked the prospect through the 7 O's, I noticed that the prospect was unusually open with me about sharing the kind of information that any typical prospect wouldn't normally share; information that exposed the real situation as it related to the sale; information about his real situation and his financial circumstances, etc.

I also noticed that the typical objections no longer existed.

There was no contention.

I found that the prospect exhibited respect for me as a person who could help him accomplish his objectives, rather than viewing me just as a "salesman."

I noticed that the prospect told me things about himself that he normally wouldn't because those things, when "given up" to a salesperson would be used as leverage against him in order to get him to buy.

I noticed that the prospect shared his excitement about buying and the results he expected to achieve.

All of this was totally and diametrically different from any other sales situation I had ever been in before. The situation truly turned from a usually "Contentious Closing" into an interestingly "Collaborative Conversation."

When I finally got to the "ask for the money" and the timing part, I thought to myself, *"OK... here's the real test. Surely this process of mine will start to show flaws. This is the money part."*

But, the prospect reacted exactly like I saw it in the Genesis Point.

Very open. No lying about the money.

He talked very frankly, even apologetically.

There was no need to discuss the sale with anyone else. There were no time constraints or delays.

Nothing.

Then came the craziest part: the prospect asked me for the sale!

I couldn't believe it.

I wrapped up the deal and had my first sale.

Then I looked down at my watch and it hit me. The whole thing had only taken a little over 45 minutes.

WOW!

This usually took over 2 hours.

The streamlining was insane to me.

The whole thing was almost surreal.

Surely this is an anomaly. There is no way that this will happen again.

I was thinking that I just got lucky on the first shot.

I sat back, took a deep breath and told the receptionist to send in the next appointment.

The experience was exactly the same.

Then the next appointment went exactly the same way – almost to the letter.

So, there I was, 32 appointments later and I had to extend my trip by three days because I was closing so much business!

Anyway, in the end I had closed 22 deals, which shrank back to 18 closed deals at $4,000 each in commissions.

I made $72,000 pure cash in commissions during that week alone.

My sales conversion ratio was over 82%.

As a salesperson that year, I made over $1.3 million in personal commissions.

The company was able to raise their initial entry investment from $14,000 to $35,000; the closing ratio went up significantly and within 90 days they were well in the black.

I continued with this organization for a few years, training their salespeople on my sales approach.

Their results were the same.

My partner and I, earned on average $400,000 - $1 Million each month in commissions from this project.

It didn't seem to matter what the salesperson's background, experience level or profile was. The format worked... every time.

And when the results were weak or off, it was easy to figure out which part of the 7 O's format the salesperson wasn't following.

I knew immediately, and that made managing and training salespeople simple.

Don't we all need that – a more efficient and effective way to keep our sales in line?

Since then I have perfected this unique selling format of mine called the 7 O's of Sales... The Intentional Experience.

I have trained every type of industry from business-to-business (b2b), to construction sales, to technology, to retail, to investments and fundraising. You name it.

I did it.

It works every single time. It doesn't matter what type of salesperson you have, and it doesn't matter what his or her deficiencies are.

It just works.

If the numbers go down, you will know exactly what is going wrong, what part of the format they are not following or using correctly.

In business and especially in sales we do not have time to figure out why the numbers are down.

With this, it's easy to know where the problem is.

When we are not performing optimally, I'm sure we can all agree that some other competitor is getting the business that is rightfully ours.

I want you to stop leaving the door open for another competitor to rob you of your sale. Is that fair enough?

So, let me train your sales personnel, every one of them and as many as you have. Old ones... brand new ones.

I'll instantly turn them into performers, as long as they will implement.

And I will give you the tools to keep them on point, performing, day in and day out.

There will be no guesswork.

Here's how the Seven O's Sales Training program works.

For years I have charged $12,000 per attendee for my knowledge and expertise taught in this program.

But as a special invitee and as a member of my unique business development format called, The CEO Society... You only need to take care of the hard cost of the program.

The cost to put on and perpetuate the two-day training. I'll waive the balance of the fee.

Before the training, each attendee will need to complete a 24 question executive profile.

Just pass out the worksheet, complete it... it's multiple choice, and send or fax it to my office.

I will have my staff process the rest of it for you.

I will cover the results of your profile during the training in great detail. This alone will amaze you.

At the training event I will cover the Seven O's in depth and you will actually customize this approach to your specific business. No generic, "one-size-fits-all" training here.

You and your staff will be proficient at using the Magic Mouth opening sales dialog before you leave.

Watch your sales stats climb the day after you leave.

Some adventurous sales people have used it on live prospects during the training, during breaks… we understand that business never stops just because you are in training.

They have seen the results improve dramatically before they left.

All in all... I can promise you that you will close more deals, for more money, faster with less hassle than ever before.

It doesn't matter if you're an old sales dog or a young pup. It doesn't matter what your background is.

It doesn't matter if you are a one-man show or a part of a multi-national sales team.

It doesn't matter if you just started in business or if you are a 3.4 billion dollar global company that's been in business for 108 years.

The Seven O's of Sales – The Intentional Experience will work for you.

So call my office... reserve your seats... send in your paperwork... and I'll see you soon.

My sincerest thanks for reading, and...

Welcome To The Money Fest.

EDward

www.ingramcontent.com/pod-product-compliance
Lightning Source LLC
Chambersburg PA
CBHW070426220526
45466CB00004B/1554